Photographic Science:

The First Two Years

by Jameson Wright

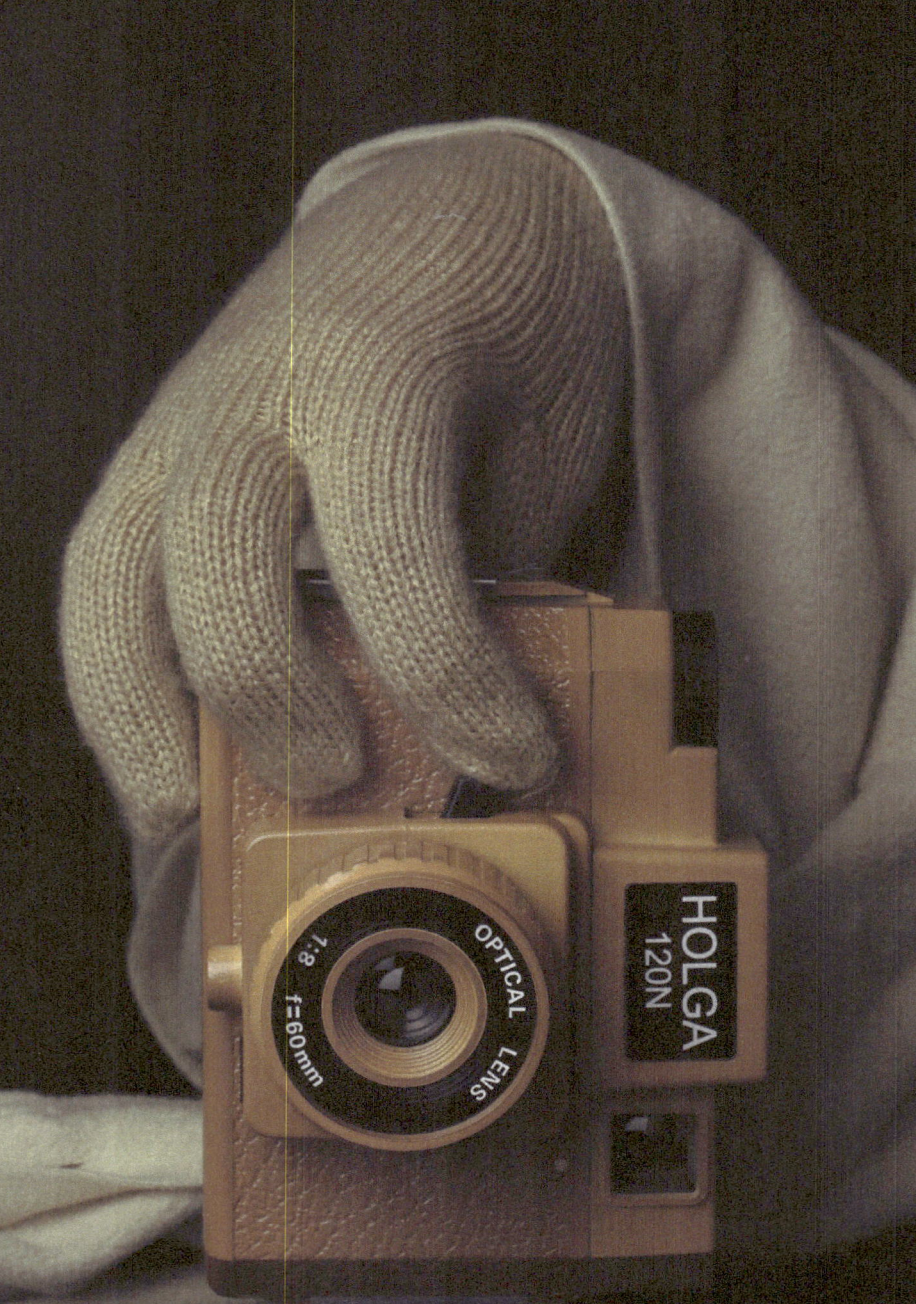

Photographic Science:

The First Two Years

by Jameson Wright

Copyright Info

All Photographs within this book were taken and processed by Jameson Wright during his first four semesters at Rochester Institute of Technology. Copyright © 2018 by Jameson Wright.

Table of Contents

Field Studio Photography for Natural Sciences....*6–8*
Stroboscopic Motion..*9–13*
Stereo Photography for Revealing Depth.........*14–19*
Infrared Photography Final Research Project...*20–32*

Assignment: Field Studio Photography for Natural Sciences

Challenges:
The biggest challenge I faced during this assignment was finding the best way to keep most of the subject fully in focus throughout all areas, seeing as how I was shooting an object with quite a bit of depth to it. In some photographs (the dead flower in particular) there were still certain areas that dropped out of focus noticeably. Another challenge I should've prepared better for was the shooting setup itself. Since I didn't have any equipment to help stabilize and standardize where the plexi-glass sheet and speedlight were placed, I just had my friend hold them in place as I placed different roses onto the sheet.

Subject:
4 different roses (all from the same bush) in different stages of life.
Scientific Classification: *Rosoideae*

Notes for Reproduction:
Have an assistant hold one of your two speedlights up underneath the plexi-glass (around an arms' length away). Make sure to synchronize the two flashes together and attach the second one to your camera. Set up your subjects onto the plexiglass and begin to find the proper exposure that will fully whiten the background without blowing out detail in the subject from the front lighting. You should be shooting vertically above your subject.

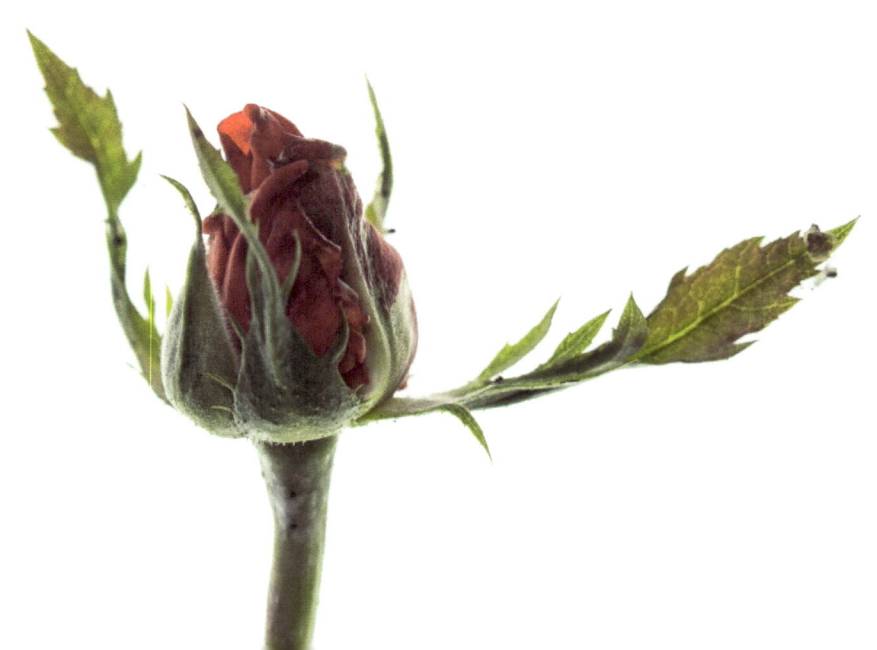

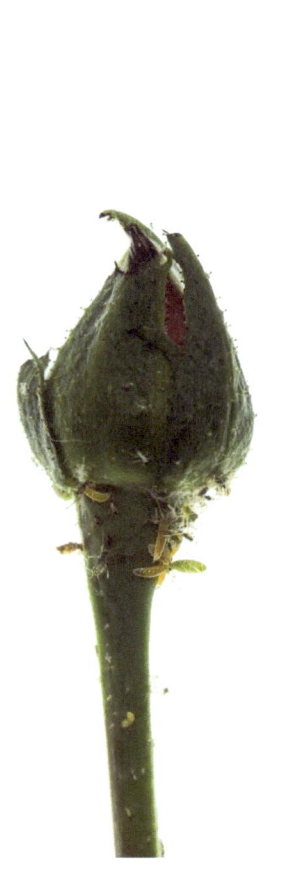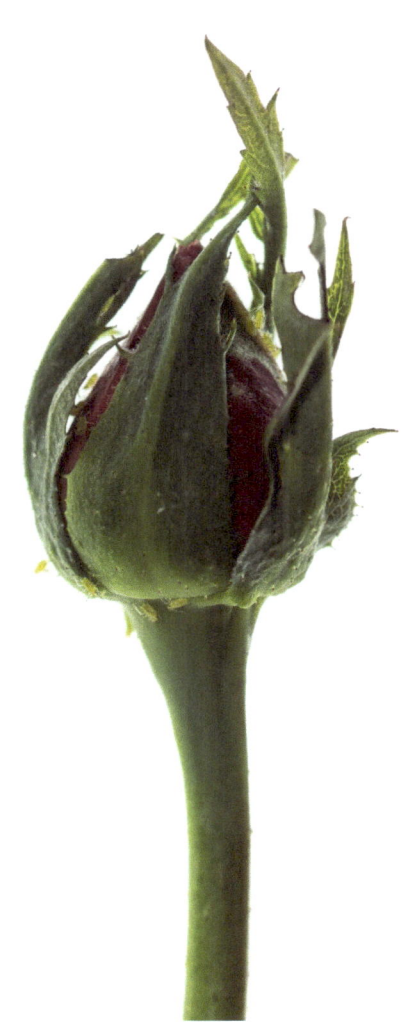

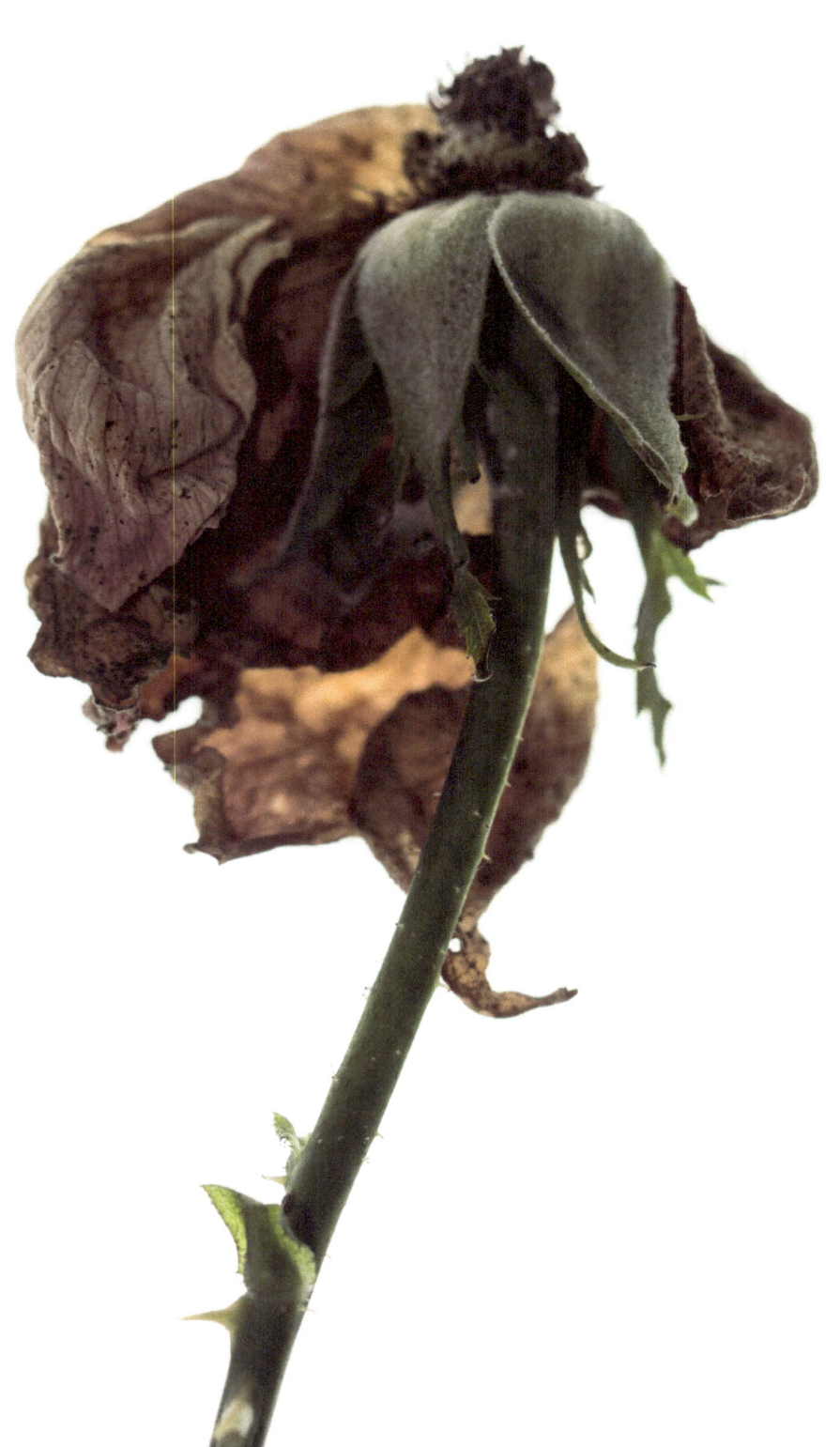

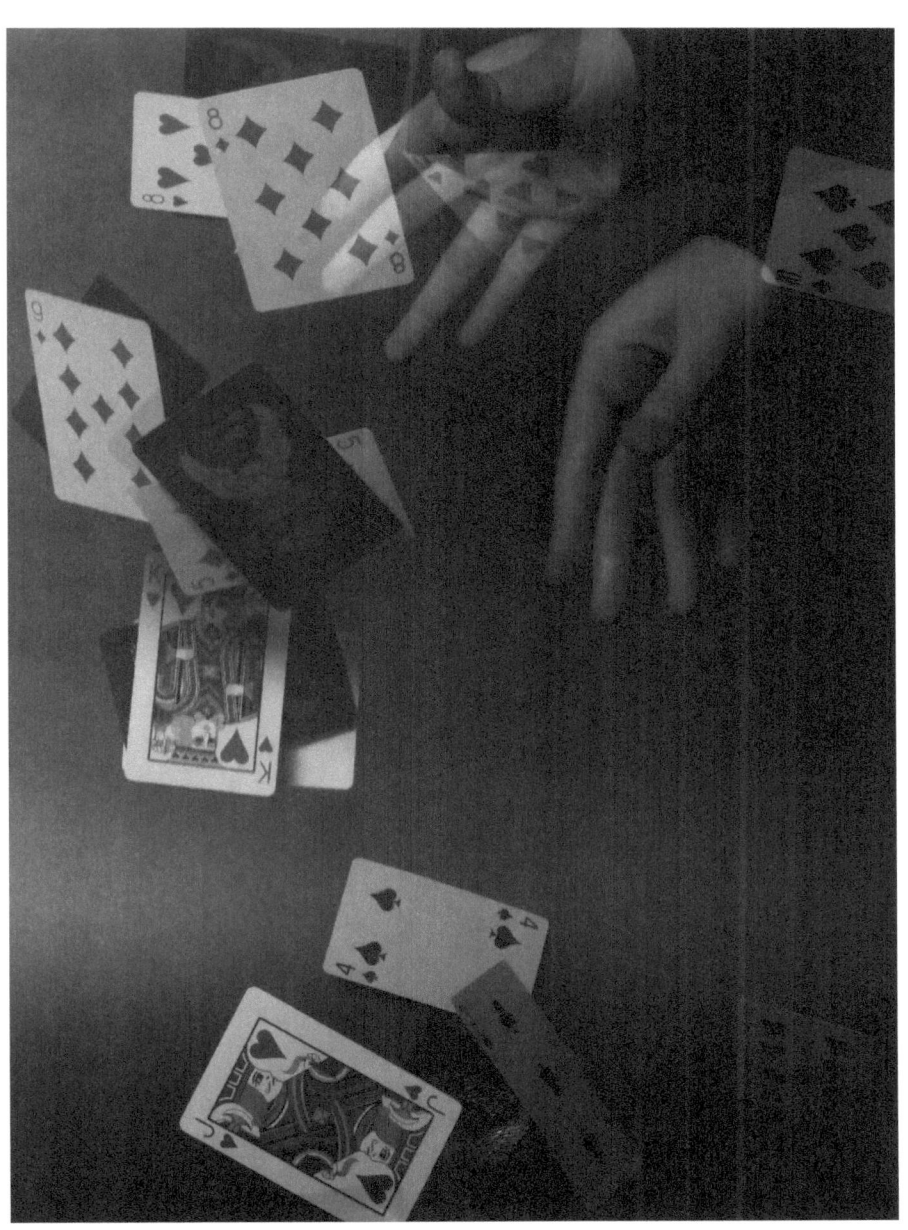

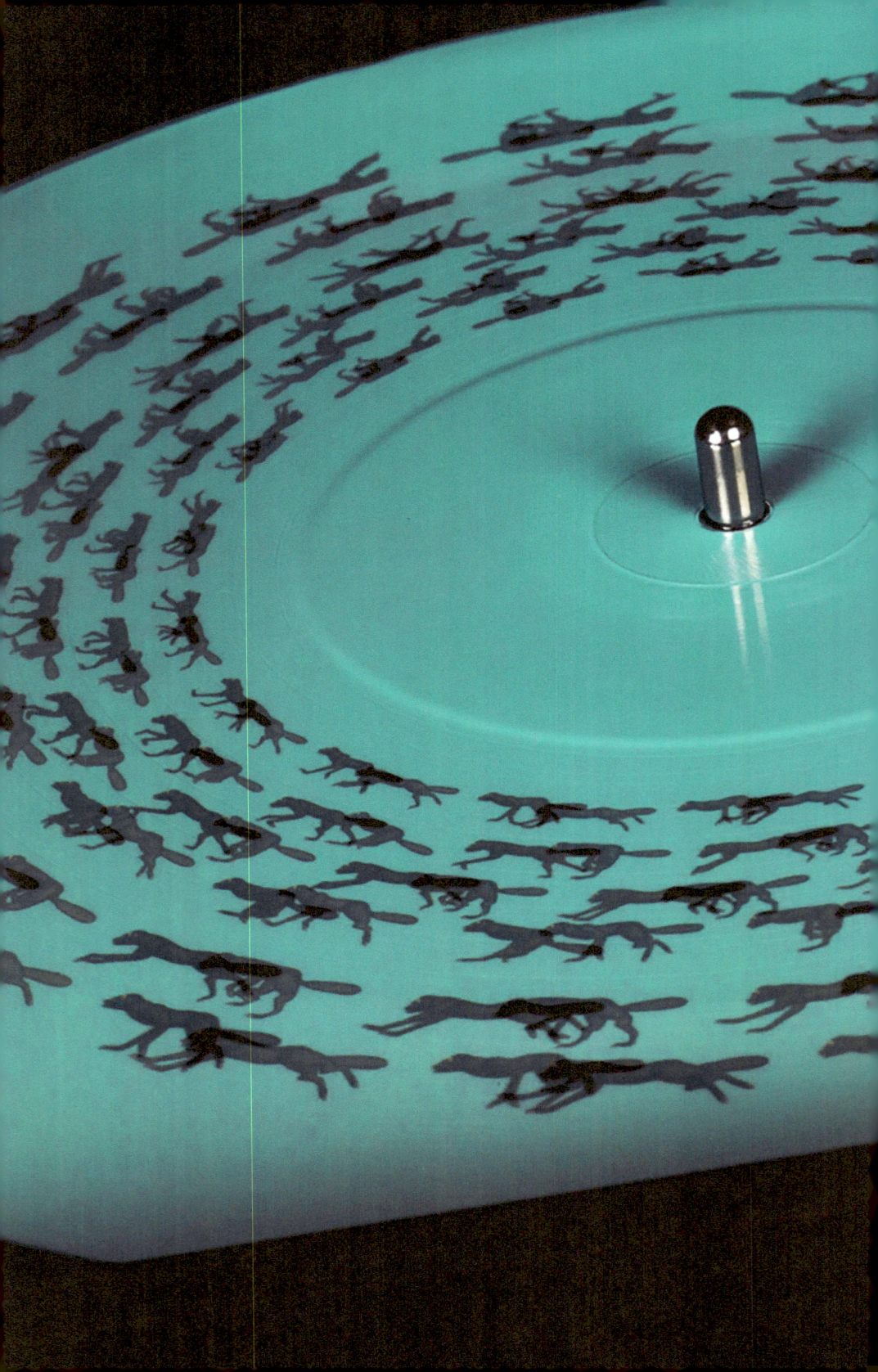

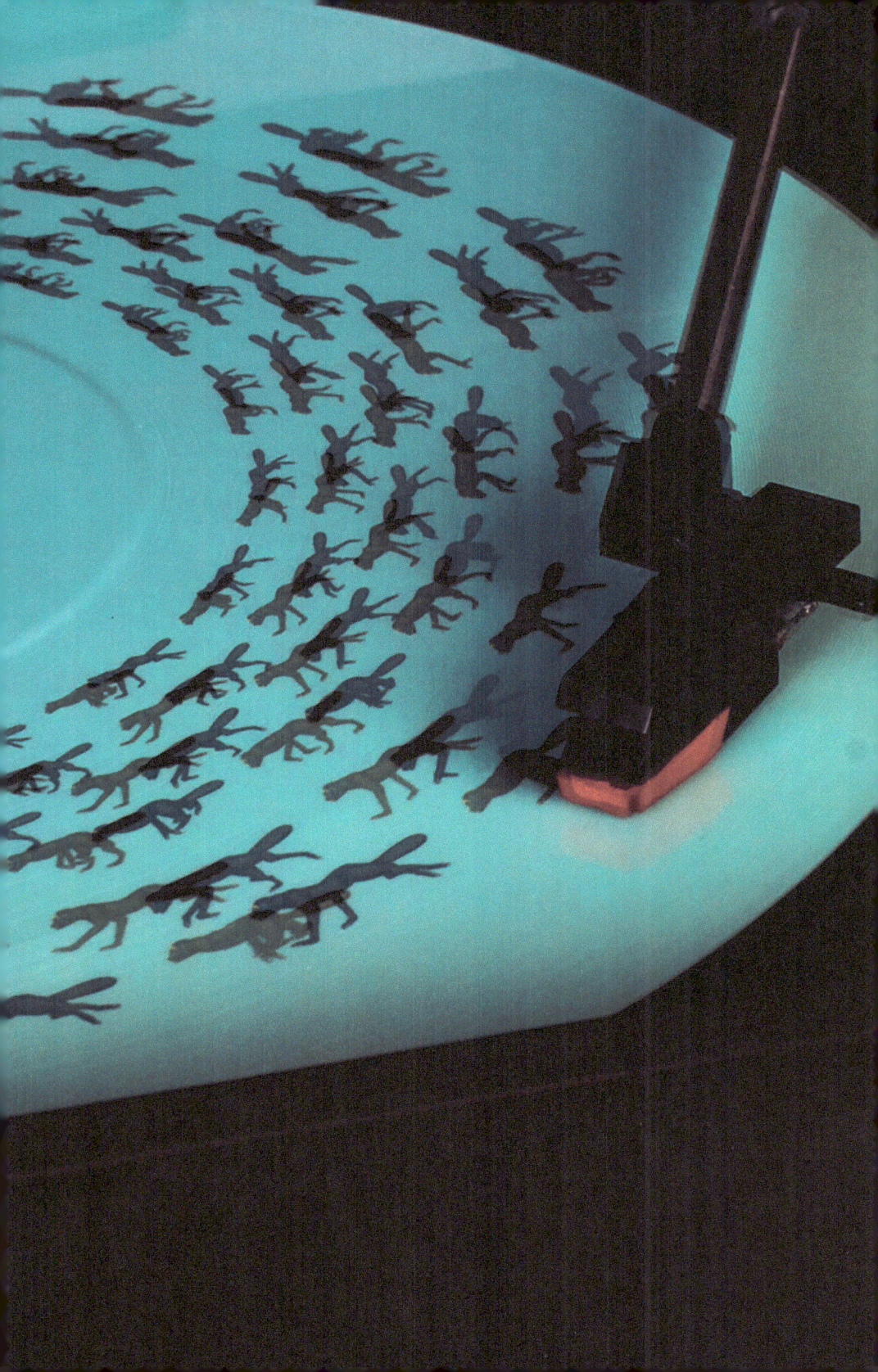

Assignment: Stroboscopic Motion

Challenges:

When attempting this assignment, I found the studio experience to be much more difficult than shooting the vinyl records spinning. The problem I ran into was how the cards were falling when shooting in the studio. Most of my frames kept turning up empty. Part of the issue with this shoot was the quickest interval available being every 0.2" because the cards were falling much quicker. Eventually to resolve this issue I had my assistant throw the cards up from within the scene, resulting in the final photograph. When shooting the vinyl records spinning with the Profoto b1 strobes, the main challenge was finding the right exposure to be able to manually fire off the 2 different lights at separate times in order to create the stroboscopic exposure. Once that was calculated it worked for almost every picture disc record I shot.

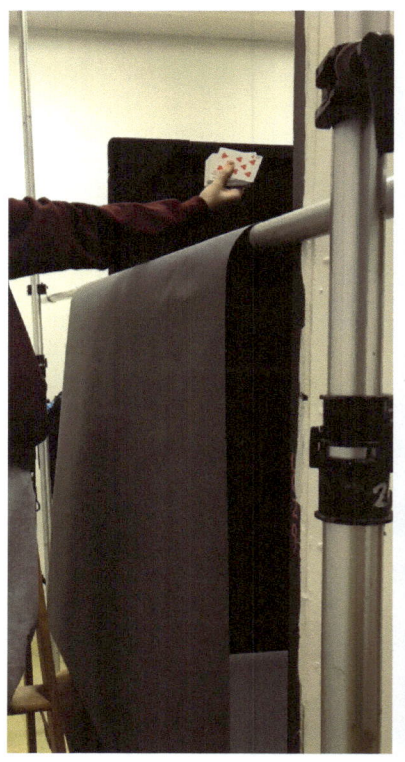

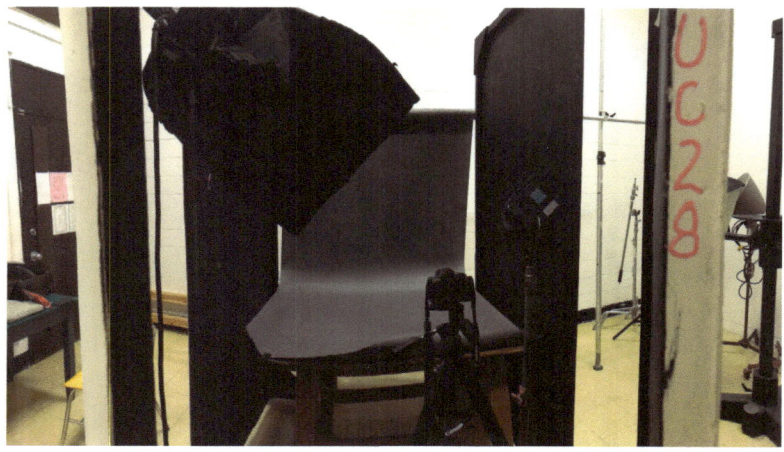

Notes For Reproduction

When shooting the vinyl records spinning:
Set up the Profoto b1 strobes in the appropriate manner, remembering to weigh down the stands due to their light weight. Once this is complete, align the scene with the record player in the proper position, with both lights roughly 45 degrees away from the camera on opposing sides. Once the proper exposure settings and power settings for the strobes has been confirmed, shoot on bulb, while having the 2 separate strobes fire off the desired amount of times one after the other. Once the desired number of strobe flashes has been fired off, close the shutter and complete the capture.

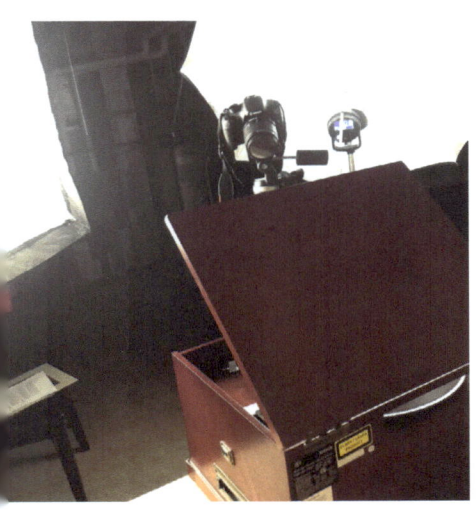
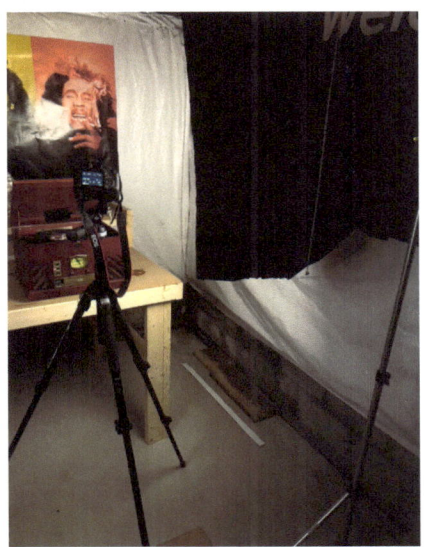

When shooting the cards in a white studio:
Set up your seamless on top of the wooden table with however many rolling walls are available with the black side facing towards your scene. Place the ladder behind the seamless in order to have an assistant drop the cards from there. Set up the proper lights illuminating the scene. After finding the proper exposure settings, set your interval and sequence to the desired setting and shoot on bulb, pressing test on the strobe pack and allowing the lights to fire off before closing the shutter.

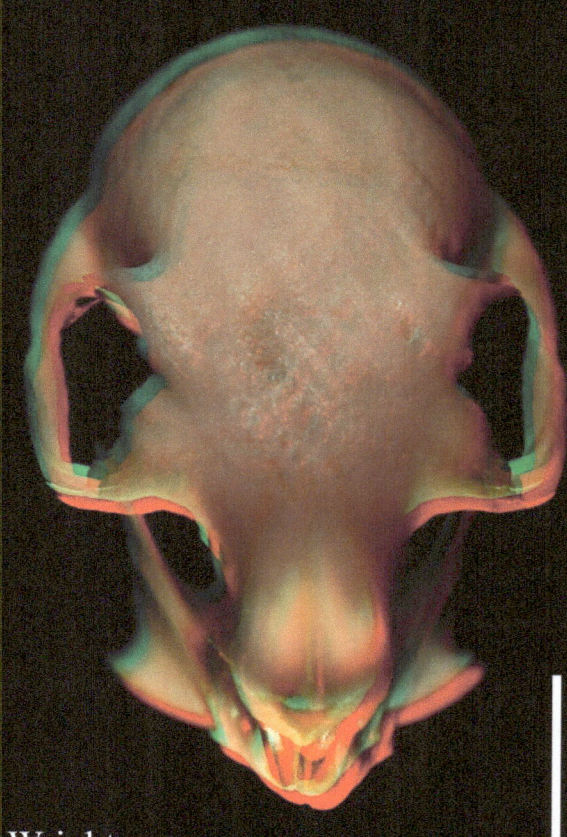

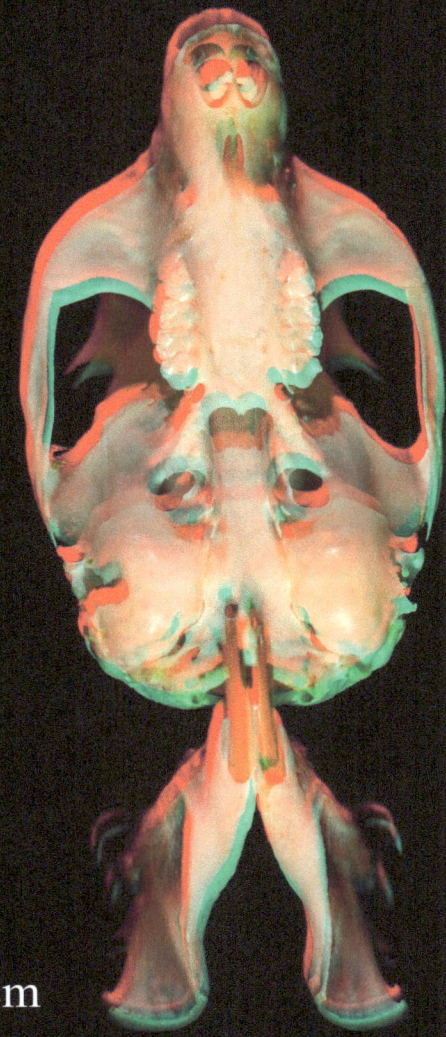

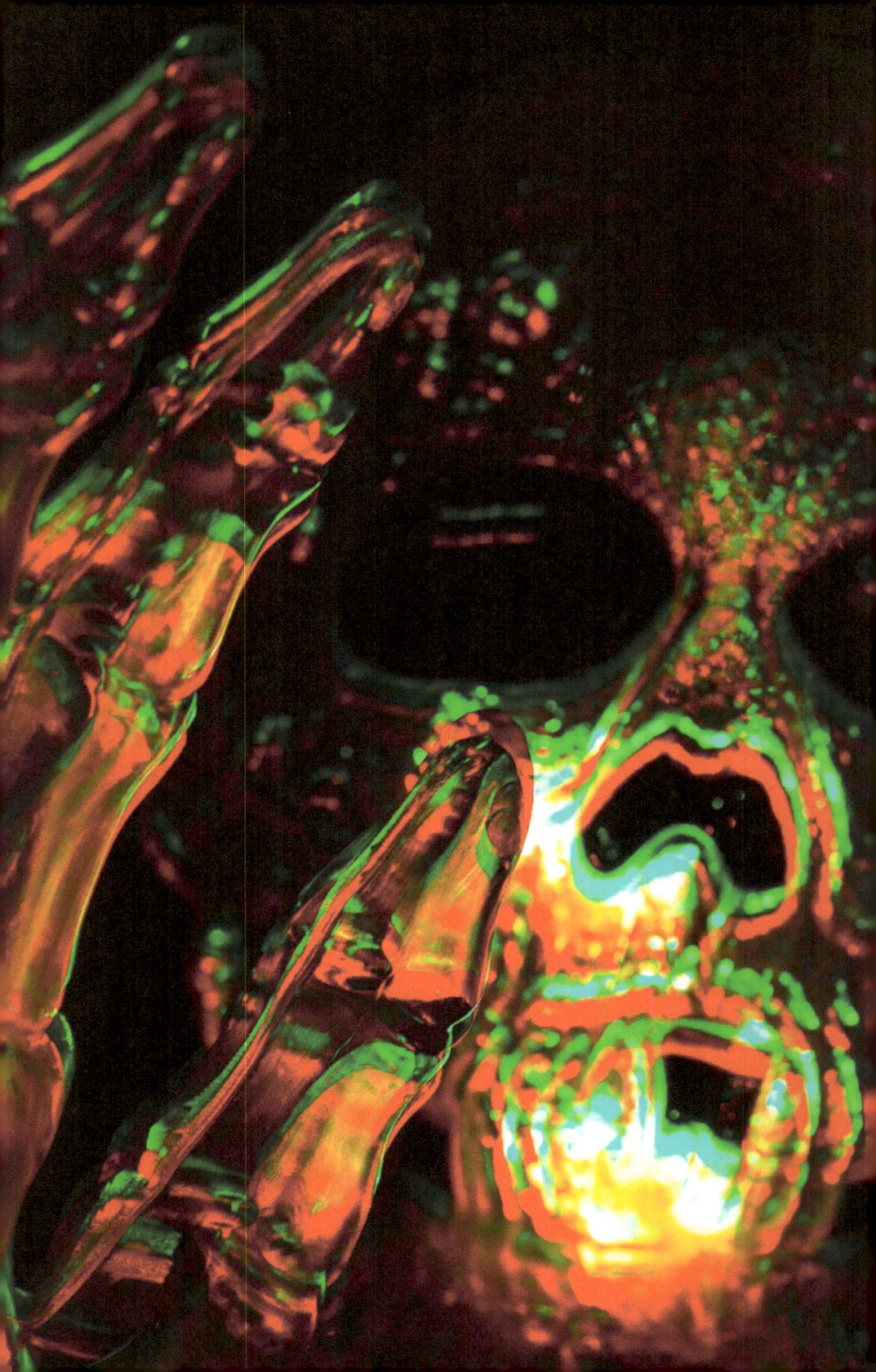

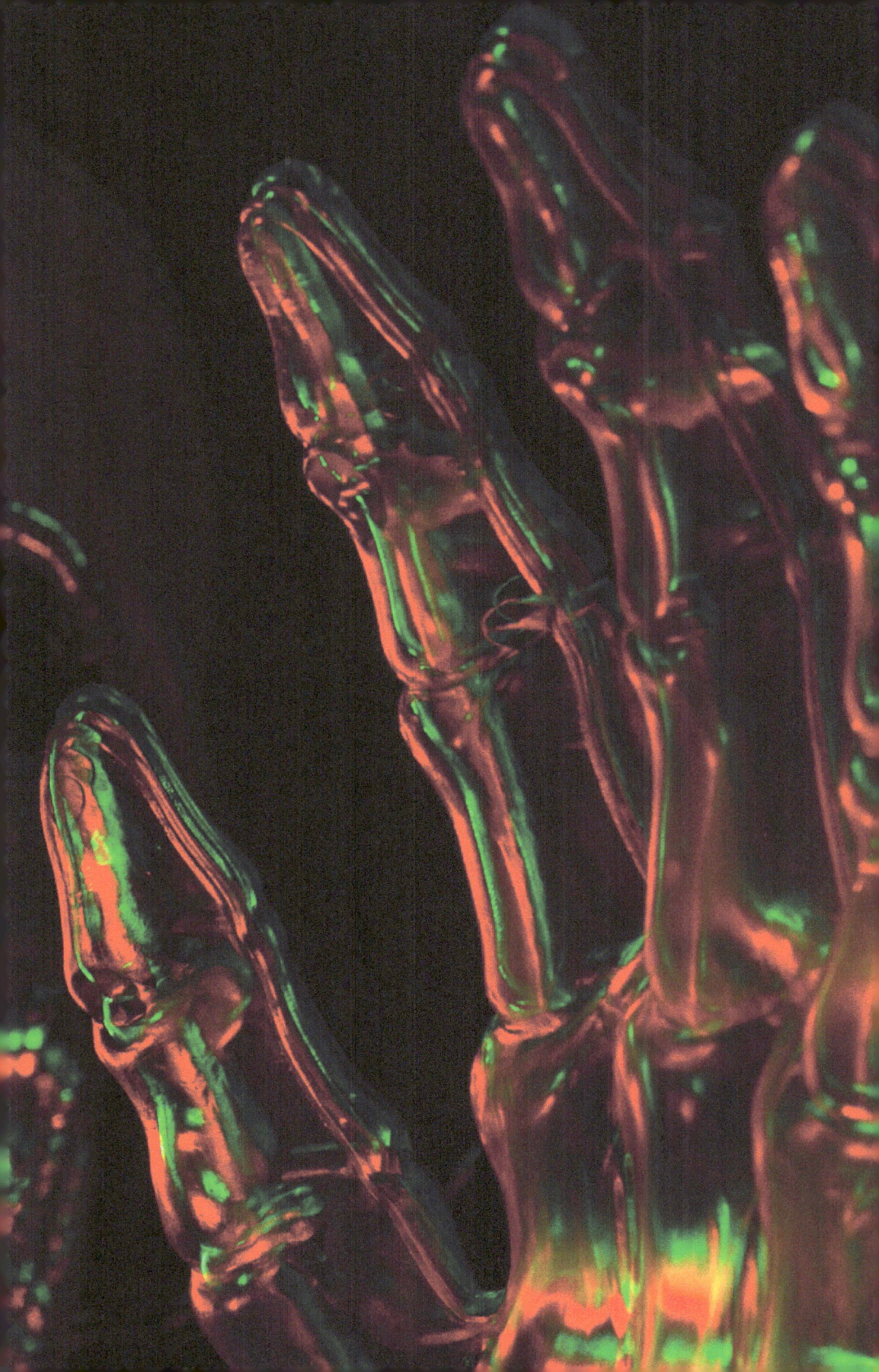

Assignment: Stereo Photography for Revealing Depth

Challenges:

When shooting the squirrel skull:
The main challenge I faced was being able to stabilize the camera on the stereo rail with the weight of the macro lens. Another challenge with shooting macro especially since the assignment revolves around depth is finding the right focus and viewpoint to capture the subject from in order to reveal the most depth in stereo anaglyph form. I much prefer the depth created from the first image (frontal view as if the lower jaw was still attached) over the second view I captured, mostly because I don't think I was able to effectively reveal the depth in the way I intended. The most challenging part with that second image was trying to reveal the stereo depth in Photoshop although I did follow the guidelines directed from the assignment. I think the error might've been because I wouldn't be able to effectively reveal the depth because of only shooting by moving the plane vertically for all of the pairs I shot instead of trying to shift from the horizontal plane. This vertical shifting approach was successful for the first image's depth though, due to the frontal positioning of the skull.

When shooting the skull decoration:
The shooting portion of this part of the assignment was not too difficult and went surprisingly well, I set up a black scene with a towel to help hide the wires and plastic stands the hands were balancing on. It was interesting photographing a subject that had its own light source inside of it. The real challenge arose when trying to create the stereo anaglyphs in Photoshop.

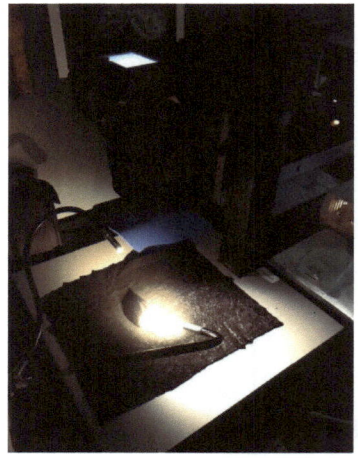

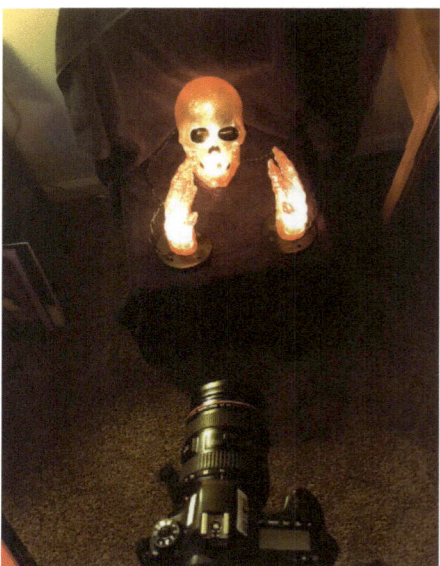

I became overwhelmed with trying to figure out how to get the depth to reveal but eventually was able to manage showing some depth.

Notes for Reproduction

When shooting a macro subject:
Have your camera with macro lens attached on a stereo rail positioned securely on your copystand with the markers on the stereo rail set to zero. Using the fiber optic lights, find the appropriate positioning for the lights, subject matter, and camera. When shooting, capture another shot at the same magnification with a ruler in frame in order to place a scale marker accurately later. Once you have the desired frame set up, measure the distance from your camera sensor to the subject [When shooting the squirrel this distance was 45 cm]. Then, calculate the disparity to be 1/30th of that distance [When shooting the squirrel, the disparity was approximately 1.5 cm] and when shooting the pair, move the sensor on the stereo rail the length of the disparity after capturing the first frame. When processing the images into a stereo anaglyph, follow the instructions on how to change the blending options to cyan and red for each of the two images (Red for left image, blue for right image).

When shooting the regular-sized subject:
Have your camera affixed securely onto a stereo rail connected to your tripod. Once you have your frame set up and ready to capture, follow the same directions on measuring the distance from your sensor plane to the subject and then calculate the disparity. The same directions apply for how to create the stereo anaglyph in Photoshop.

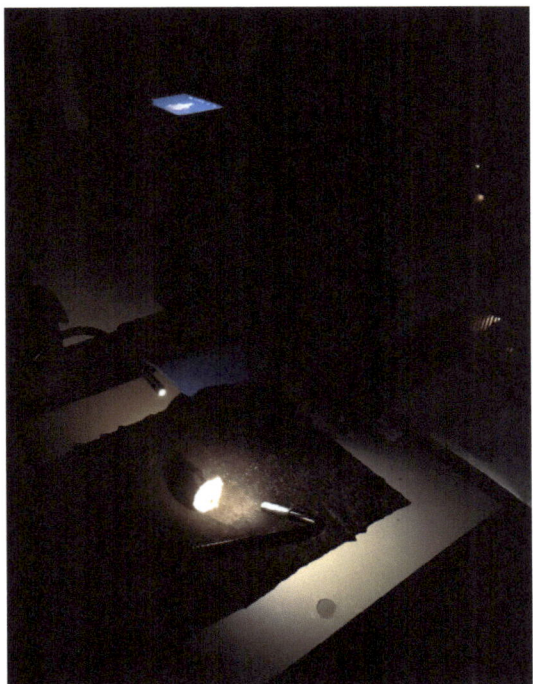

Photography II Final Project & Infrared Research Project

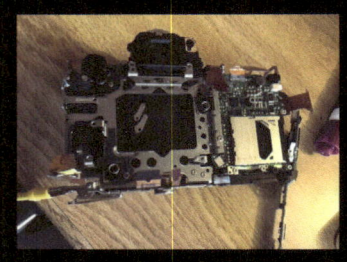

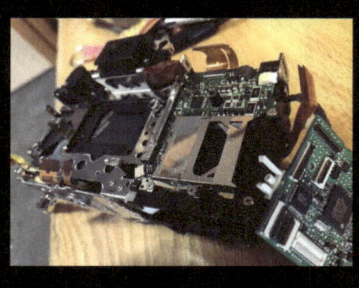

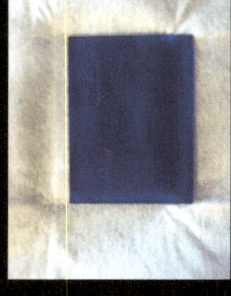

My final project for Photography II was to research and execute the process of manually converting the sensor of a Canon Rebel T1i to only view and record infrared wavelengths and blue light wavelengths. Selections of Infrared photographic works from my Photo Research Project shot during Spring Break 2017 are also included to display the levels of creative freedom shooting in infrared provides.

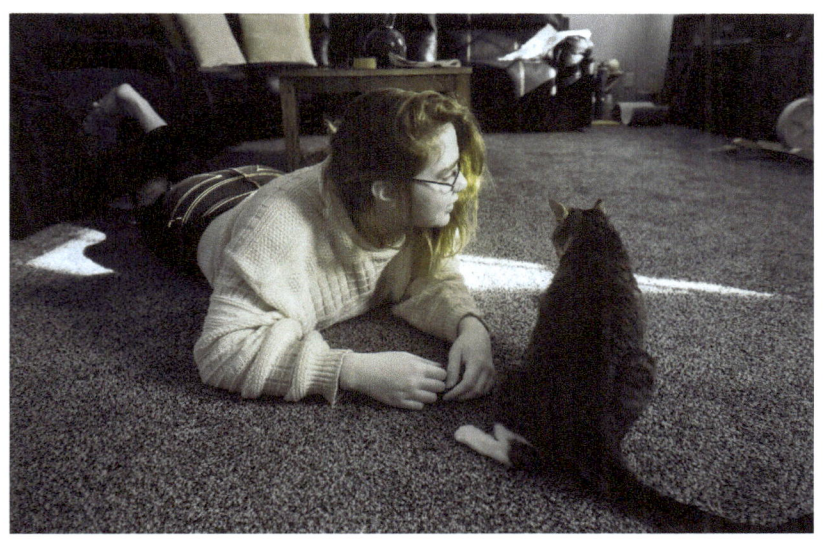

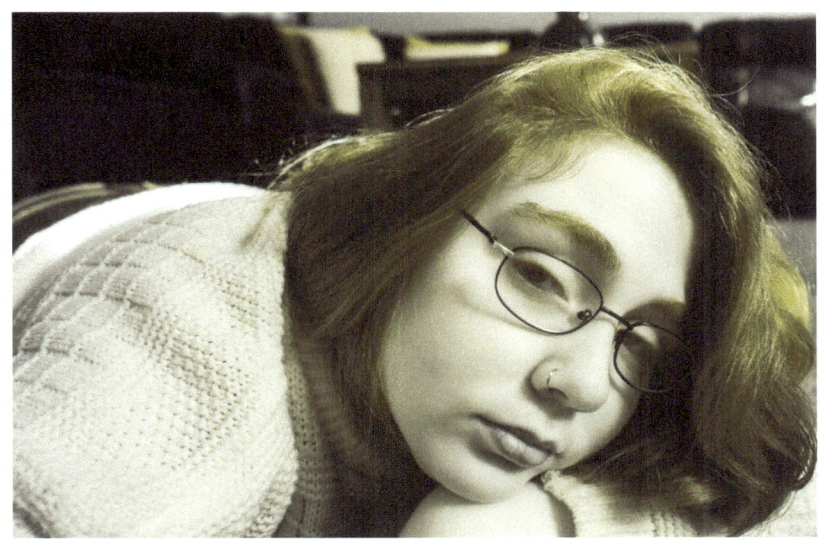

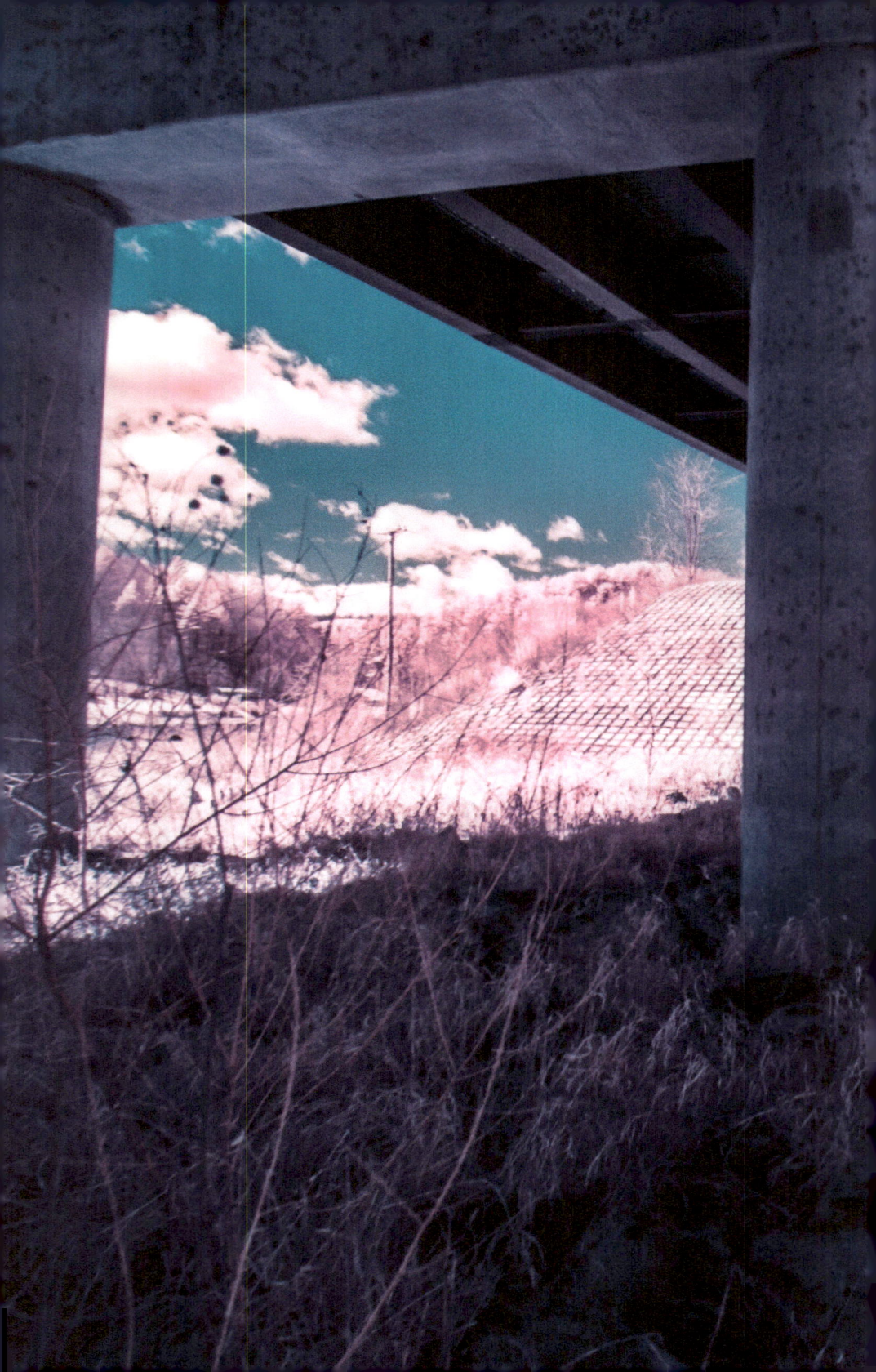

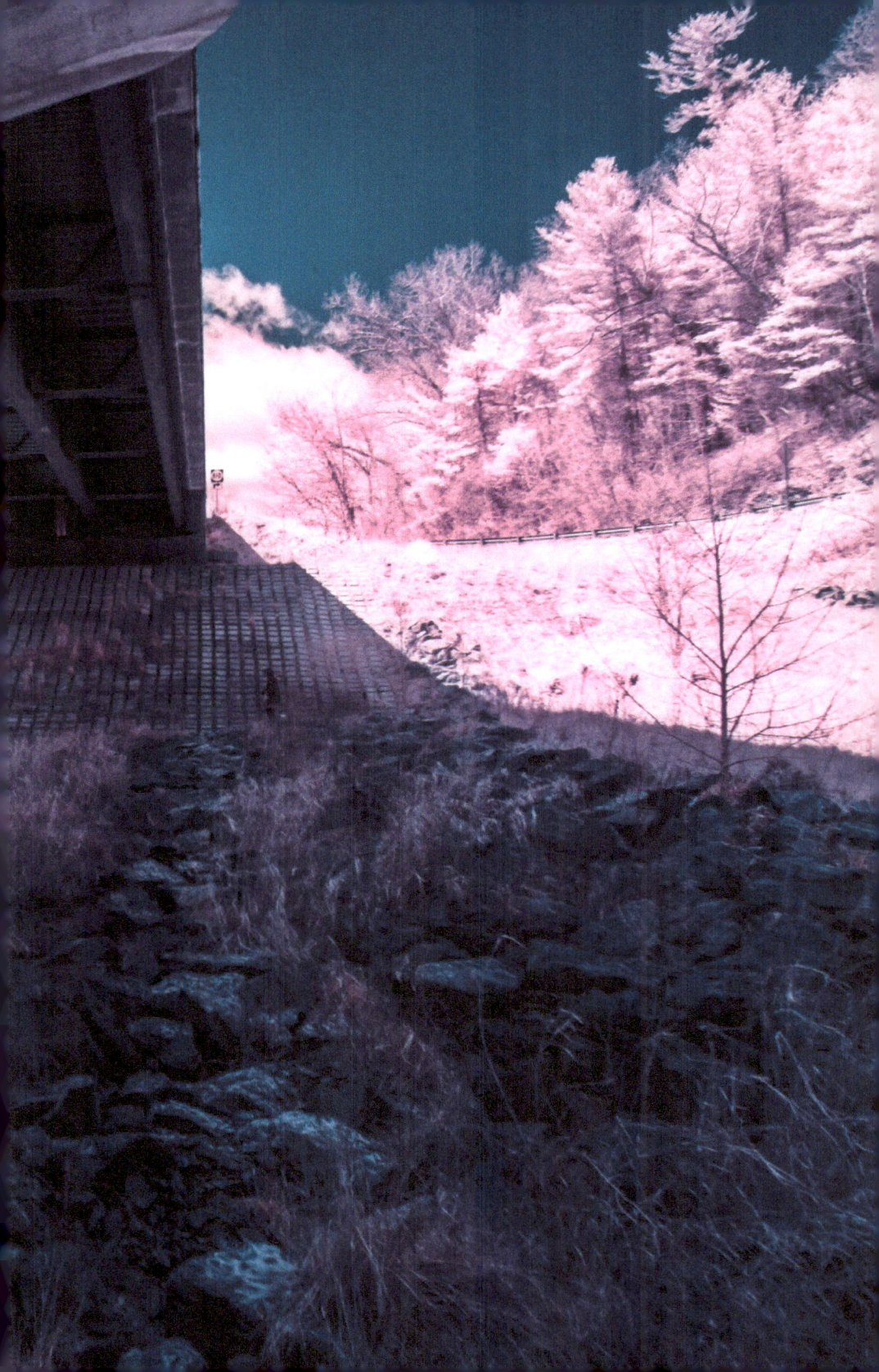

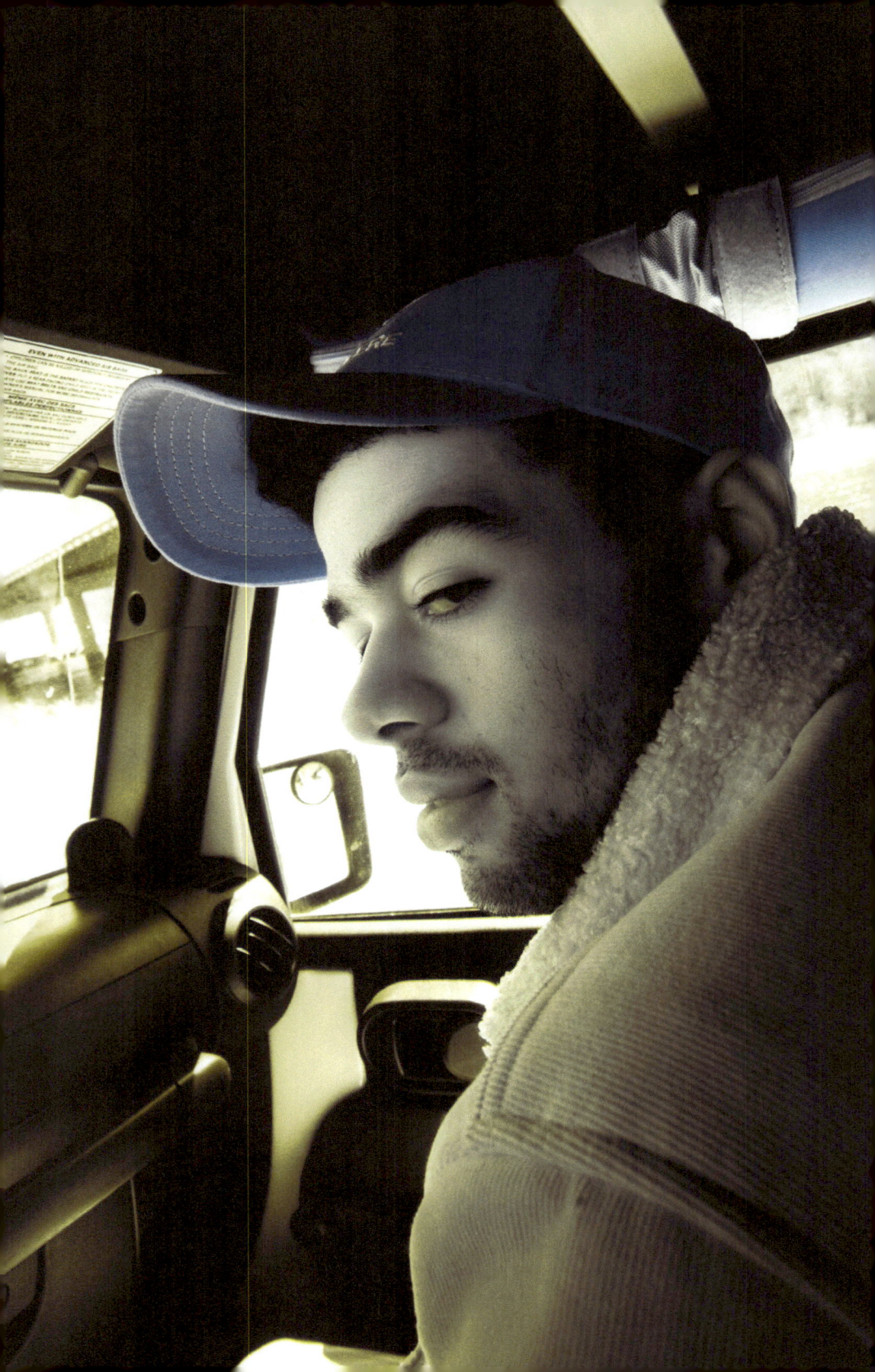

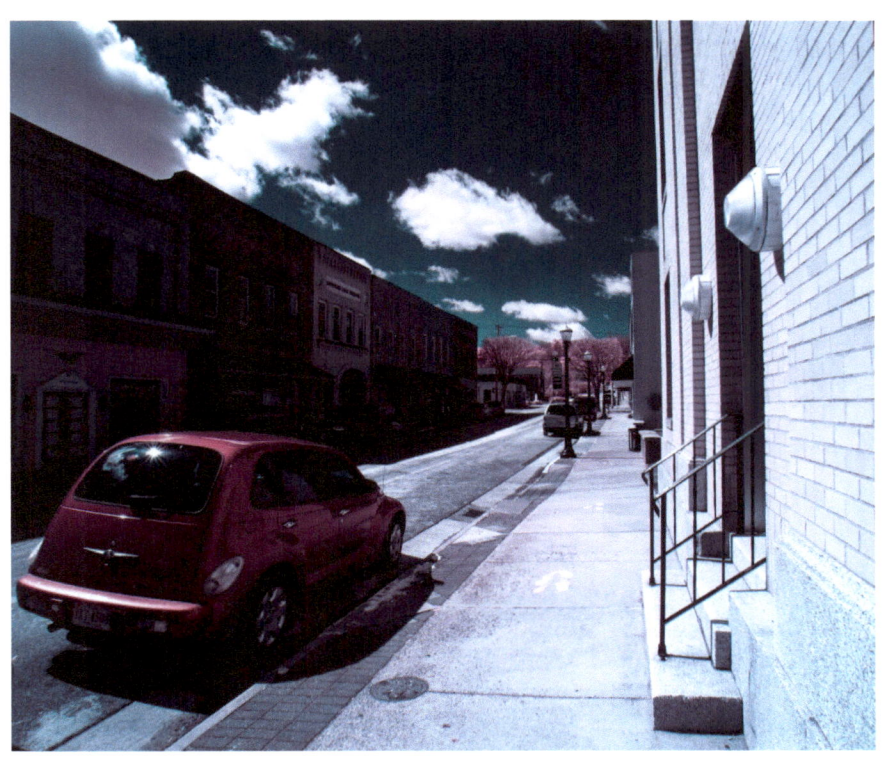

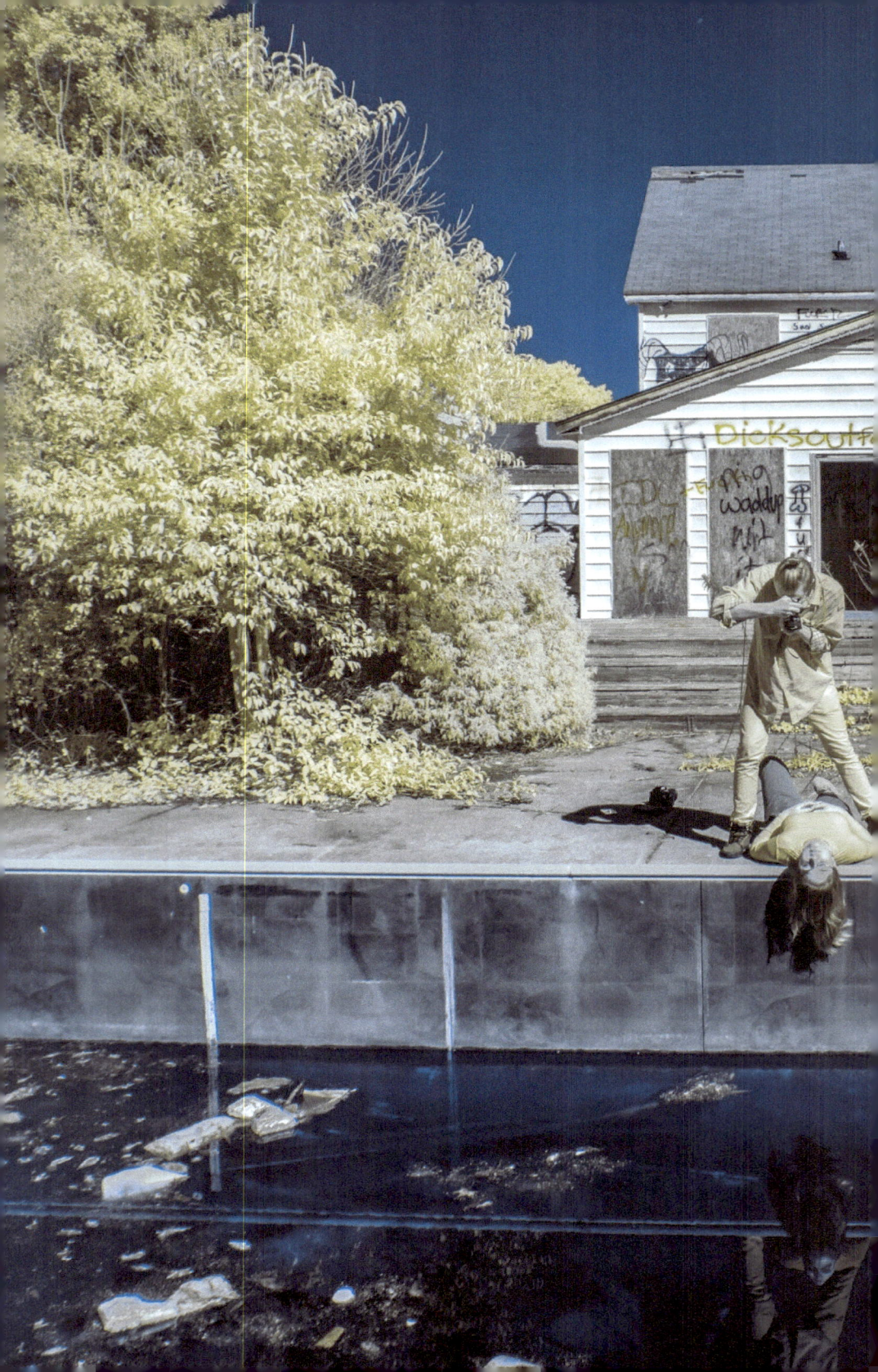

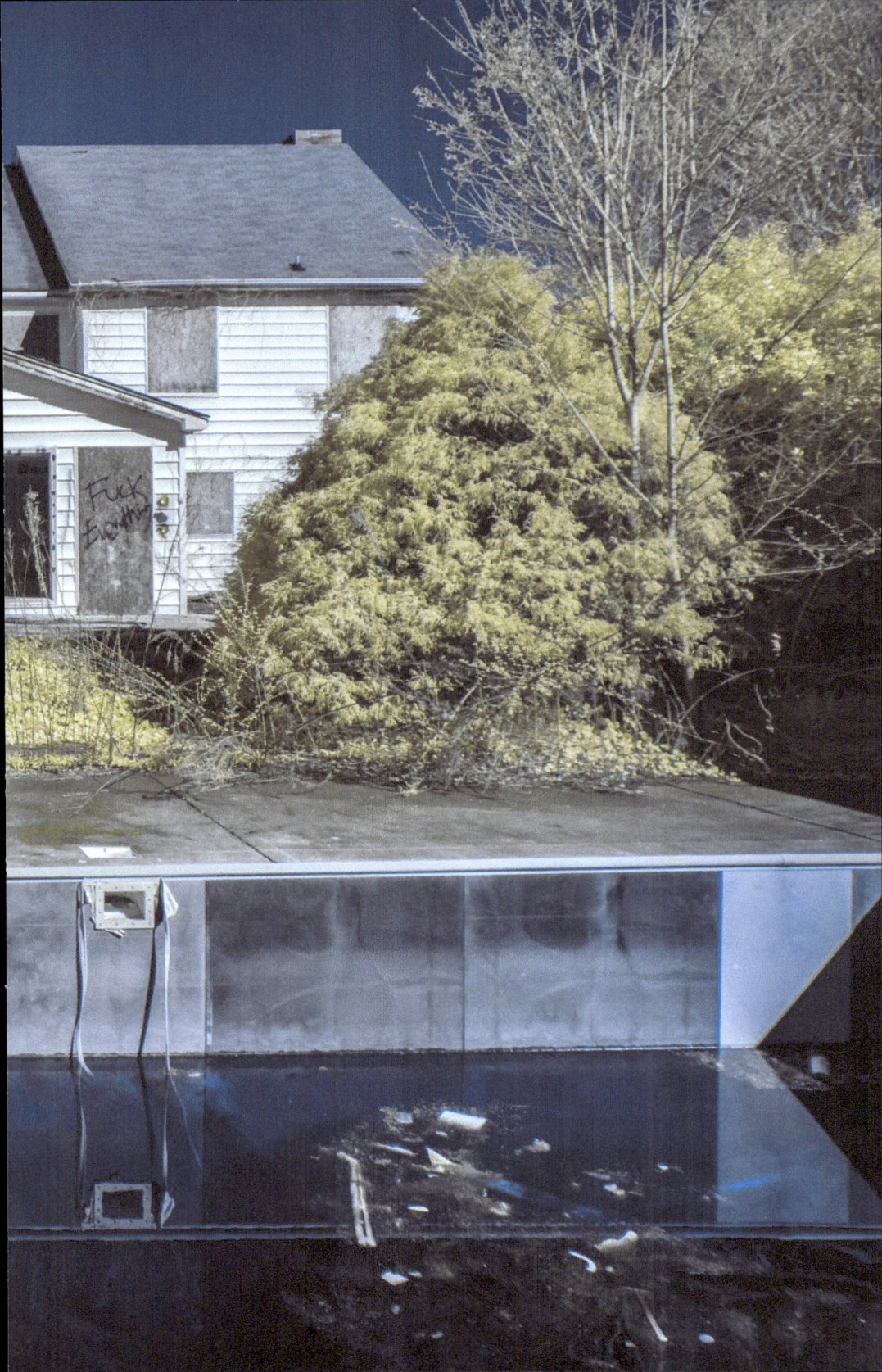

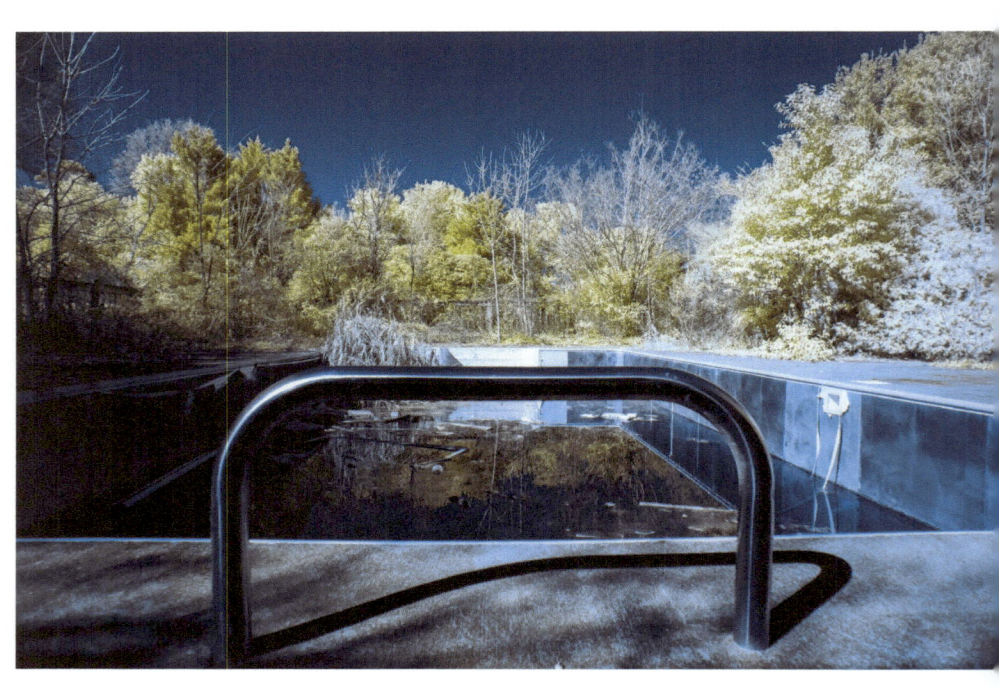

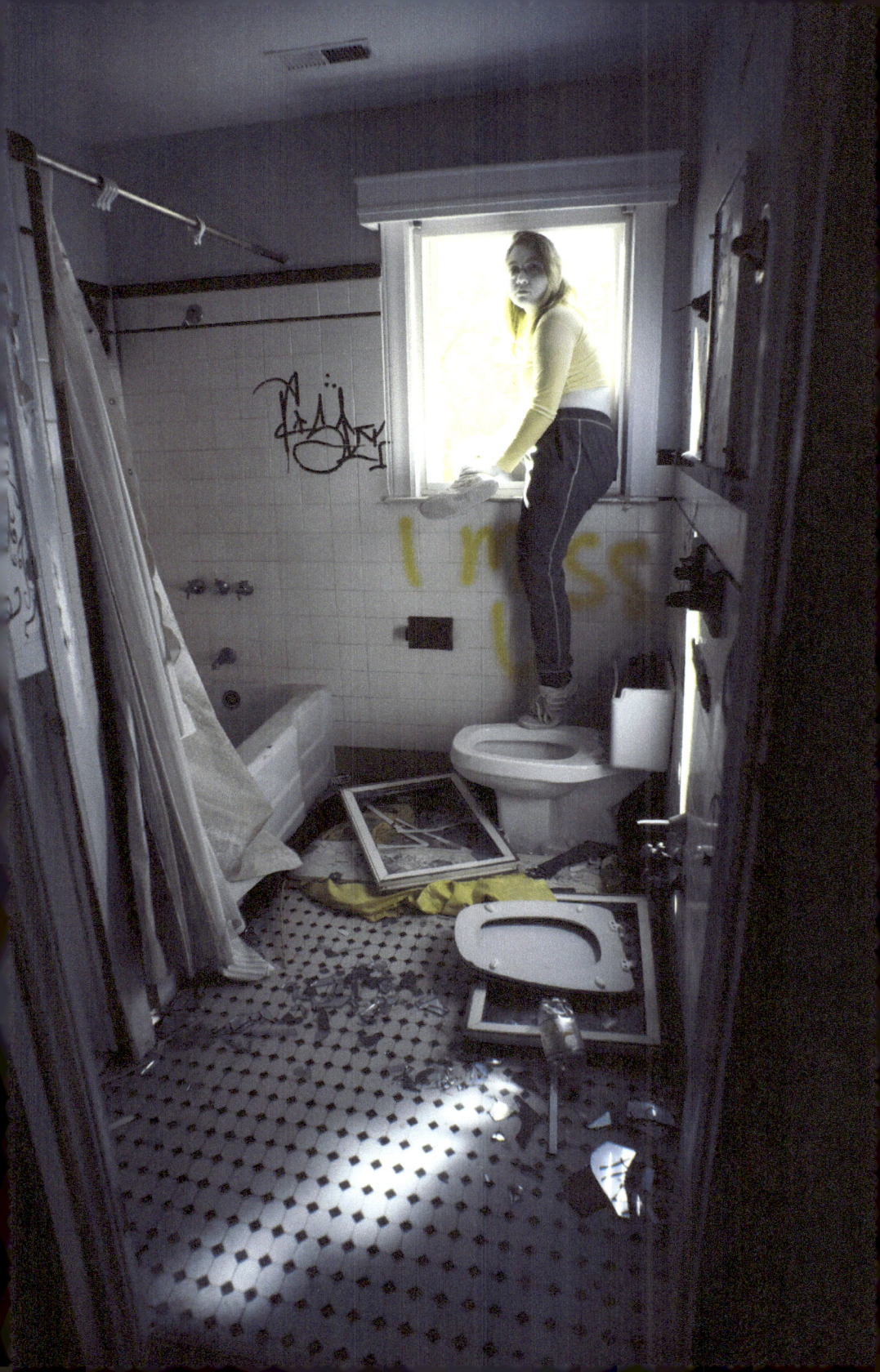

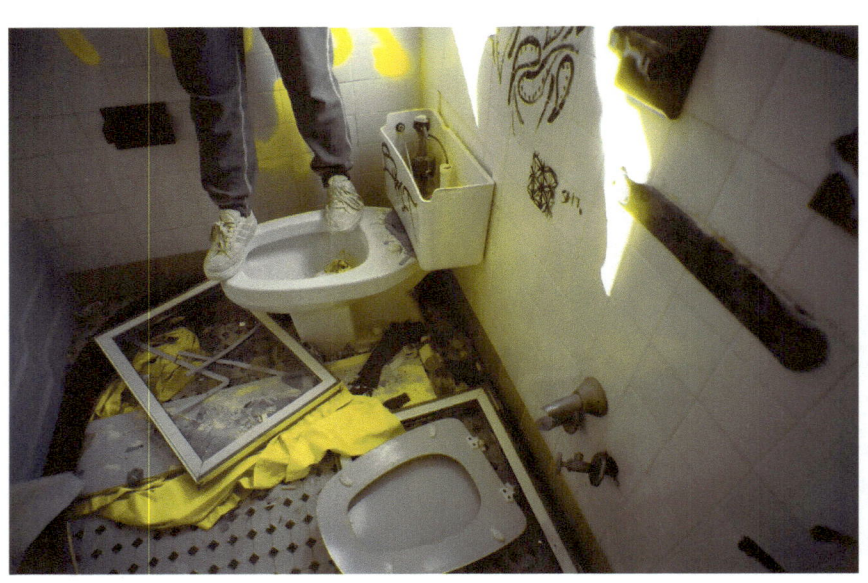

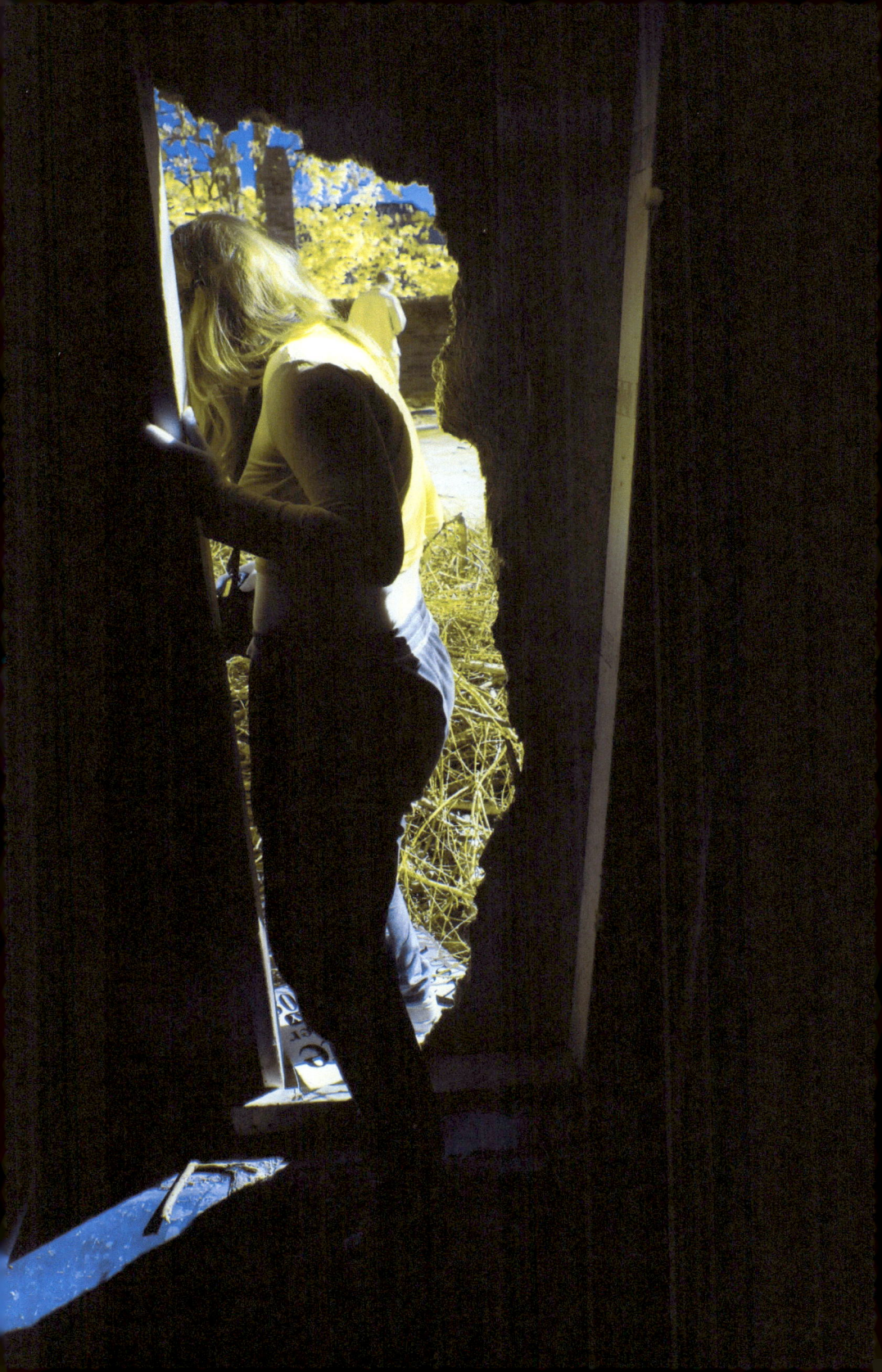

Colophon

The typeface used throughout this book consists only of Optima with the bold, italic, bold italic, and Extra-Black versions included as well. Various point sizes were used in the book that include 10-on-12 and 11-on-13 for text bodies. The copyright info, table of contents, and this colophon are 12 point font. This book was printed by
CreateSpace, an Amazon Company.

www.ingramcontent.com/pod-product-compliance
Lightning Source LLC
Chambersburg PA
CBHW040343220526
45473CB00009B/2777